One Night Stand

Principles for Avoiding the Pitfalls of Ungodly
Relationships and Setting the Stage for Successful
Marriages and Families

Pastor John F. Ramsey Sr.

All Scripture is taken from the American Standard Version Bible. Accessed on Bible Gateway. www.BibleGateway.com.

Sermon To Book
www.sermontobook.com

One Night Stand / John F. Ramsey Sr.
ISBN-13: 978-1-945793-49-3
ISBN-10: 1-945793-49-X

I dedicate this book to my wife, Alicia.

Alicia, I thank you for all the years you've believed in me and served, encouraged, and supported me in everything God has called me to do. Many of the principles in this book reflect the blueprint that we used while dating and throughout our marriage. Thank you for encouraging me to dream and not to settle for anything less than God's best for my life, our family, and our ministry.

It is my prayer that the practical principles I have applied over the last twenty-five years will empower and encourage every person who reads this book.

CONTENTS

The Recipe for Love 3

Offering Your Best 9

Shedding Shame 19

Raising the Standards 31

Prepare To Be Picky 43

Stay United 57

Live Holy… Even When You're Tempted 71

Master Your Money 85

Work Together 99

Raise Them Right 111

God Is the Glue 123

Notes 127

About the Author 129

About Sermon To Book 132

The Recipe for Love

My people are destroyed for lack of knowledge: because thou hast rejected knowledge.

—Hosea 4:6

Do you dream of love that binds everything together in perfect harmony? Have you found yourself desperately searching for such an experience? Perhaps you believe you have found it; perhaps you're thinking of marrying the love of your life.

But with marriage being what it is today, how can you be sure?

Love, True Love

We are living in the world of fast food, fast money, and fast "love." I put "love" in quotation marks here, because a love that is rushed, overly emotional, and chaotic is not the real thing.

Sadly, the English language doesn't have many words to express a strong, positive emotion or feeling. The best we can do is to say that we "love" someone, but because of our limited vocabulary on this topic, we also have to apply the word "love" to other things and experiences. So, we love ice cream, walks on the beach, our brothers and sisters, our country, our jobs, and we also love God.

The things that should not be compared as equal, such as ice cream and God, tend to be lumped together as things we "love."

I believe that this plays tricks on our psyche.

In Greek, there are four different words used to describe the feeling of love:

Philia means the connection of friendship, or brotherly love.

Storge is an affection that characterizes the relationships between parents and children or other family members.

Eros is used for sensual desire.

Agape is the love of God for man and of man for God.[1]

Four words provide four completely different meanings for this very complex and incredible emotion that we call "love." For us today, we tend to seek a "fast love." We chase infatuation, self-absorption, shallow interactions, or casual sex, and yet these are not the fulfilling, meaningful things that our hearts truly desire. We chase *eros* and we fill our lives with *philia* when what we really need and are searching for is *agape.*

Whether you are a follower of Christ or a nonbeliever with similar principles, you must realize that a foundation for a long-term, happy relationship requires preparation and hard work on yourself first—you must already realize this, otherwise you wouldn't have picked up this book! Then, you must understand that a close collaboration with your partner takes time and effort and patience, as well as understanding and forgiveness.

Love between man and wife—commitment between the two—is not easy to come by. It is not found in a one-time sensual evening or a moment of bliss. It is a journey—a journey that you take together.

Head Knowledge

Like any meaningful relationship, a happy, long-lasting marriage has to be built, worked on, and cherished, but this journey can be made easier with the right guidance.

Hosea 4:6 warns us that a lack of knowledge can destroy us, and this is true within the bonds of marriage, as well. Ignorance is not bliss. Not understanding how true *agape* love works in true relationships can lead you into unhappiness and misery.

Not knowing the how, what, where, when, and why within a marriage can set any relationship on a destructive course.

This book hopes to change that. Just as you have picked it up to work on yourself in preparation for marriage or in anticipation of a serious relationship, you can also expect to have your knowledge base strengthened. The application-focused workbook sections at the end of each chapter will help you develop a greater understanding of the various aspects of a blessed, harmonious relationship.

This book will show you how to best prepare for life in love and harmony. It will help you avoid the pitfalls of ungodly, unhappy dating, whether you are a single person preparing to enter the dating game, or you're a seasoned "dater" who is tired of fruitlessly searching for your perfect mate. It will also help the brides- or grooms-to-be.

I've Been There

Twenty-two years into my marriage, I can tell you I've been there and done that. I've seen the good times and the hard times. I've loved my wife through sickness and health, for better or for worse richer and poorer. My marriage has experienced incredible happiness and immense strain.

My wife and I have two lovely children—one of them with special needs—who are both fulfilling God's calling on their lives while in college. We have spent years serving the Lord in churches and helping young couples start their marriages off the right way, with God at the center. I've counseled couples, helped marriages, and done everything I can to salvage these precious relationships.

From these years of experience, I know what works and what doesn't. I know what makes a marriage journey a bit easier and what doesn't. And I know how to instill this knowledge that I've acquired into your own marriage and your own relationship. Everything I know is packed into this book.

I encourage you to put these principles into play immediately. Treat this as a guidebook rather than just another quick read to breeze through once and toss aside. Respond thoughtfully and prayerfully to the reflection questions in the workbook section after each chapter, and challenge yourself to live out the action steps. Commit to implementing the knowledge this book will impart into your daily life.

You will see change. You will receive clarity. You will know how to strengthen your relationship.

Fairy tales conventionally end with the words "They lived happily ever after," but no one ever tells you exactly how "happily ever after" happens. And no, it doesn't "just happen" because of love. Yes, love is important, but it certainly isn't enough to get you through decades of highs and lows and everything in between.

Dating is easy. You meet someone who is fun, attractive, and agreeable, and you go out and have a good time. You pursue a relationship. But finding your true mate—the person with whom you can spend the rest of your life—is much harder. And the act of marriage certainly doesn't make it any easier. It requires an ongoing effort to stick together, regardless of life's trials.

I want you to achieve the dream of experiencing the "love, which is the bond of perfectness" (Colossians 3:14). I want you to have unchanging, trustworthy, embracing love and happiness in your marriage.

I want you to cleave to your spouse and "be one flesh" (Genesis 2:24).

If you are ready to take this path, too, turn the page and discover the recipe for a God-centered, principle-driven relationship and strong marriage.

CHAPTER ONE

Offering Your Best

And God saw everything that he had made and, behold, it was very good.

—Genesis 1:31

It's sad to see people expecting others to fill holes in their lives, to add meaning to their existence, to heal their wounds. This is a recipe for another broken heart. Unfortunately, I see this a lot in young relationships. Both parties feel as though they need the other person to achieve happiness or popularity or success.

A relationship is not a way to fill a void! In fact, the opposite is true. A healthy relationship is the result of two people who have become rooted in who they are and what their calling is as individuals. In other words, we need to have our own lives, our own identities, clear and whole before we will have a successful relationship with another person.

Don't wait for a husband to start living. Paris is still Paris if you go there by yourself. Don't wait for a wife to bring meaning to your life; you've got to have your own identity before you get out there, looking for another person to join you on your journey through life.

Learn to appreciate the value of who you are as a human being. This is the first key to happily-ever-after. Value yourself and your existence. View yourself as a child of God. Be happy with yourself, and a happy relationship will follow.

Love Yourself First

Any relationship is comprised of two people, representing one half of the relationship. So, what happens if the half that you provide is broken and needy and searching for wholeness? What happens if the other person also provides a damaged, unstable half? It's a recipe for disaster!

While you can't control others, you can certainly control yourself and what you bring into a relationship. This is why it's so important to learn how to get along with yourself before you expect to get along with anybody else.

But sadly, many singles skip this step. They don't stay dateless very long, and they jump from relationship to relationship while they remain clueless as to how to enjoy their own company.

God created you the way you are, and you are beautiful and good in God's eyes—and that is all that counts. The movies, TV shows, and video clips from our modern society are what make us think that being a size 0 is beautiful or that you have to have white skin or long legs or broad shoulders and a six-pack.

This is not how God sees you, and it's not how you should see yourself. God knows everything about you; there are no secrets from Him. More importantly, He loves everything about your personality and your looks. This is how it should be in your relationship. You should love and accept yourself as God loves and accepts you, and your significant other should feel the same way. If there is any pressure for you to lose weight or change an aspect of your personality or be something other than what God made you to be, then that is not the right person for you.

Give Your All

Not only do you have to love and accept yourself and be confident in who you are in Christ, another important component of a meaningful relationship is that you should be willing to give your all to that other person, even when you don't feel as though you have anything left to offer.

Do you remember this scene?

And he sat down over against the treasury, and beheld how the multitude cast money into the treasury: and many that were rich cast in much. And there came a poor widow, and she cast in two mites, which make a farthing. And he called unto him his disciples, and said unto them, Verily I say unto you, This poor widow cast in more than all they that are casting into the treasury: for they all did cast in of their superfluity; but she of her want did cast in all that she had, even all her living.
—Mark 12:41–44

Pay attention to how excited Jesus was by this woman's small gift. This was a woman who was loved completely by God, and it was clear that she loved Him back. Yet she chose to give even more of herself to Him. She gave the last bit that she had. It didn't amount to much by the world's standards, but it was enough to leave an incredible impact on Jesus, because it symbolized her giving her *all.*

No, in a dating relationship, you don't have to give your very last cent, but you must be willing to make sacrifices! In marriage, though, it's a completely different story. You must always give your all. You must push to give more and more of yourself, even when it's not pleasant or when it means making a huge sacrifice.

Without giving, there is no real love.

Don't misunderstand, though. There can be limits on how much you should give, because you can't let other people make you their source for need fulfillment, either. A relationship that is healthy and worth pursuing to the end is one that is mutually beneficial. If you're in a relationship that doesn't make you a better person, then you may want to rethink that relationship. Spouses don't fill our needs; rather, they bring out the best in us. Keep that in mind as you weigh how much you are giving to your relationship.

Take Care of You

It's never too late to take care of you. You may have a broken heart. You may be stuck in a relationship in which you're giving so much more than you are getting. You may have a hard time seeing yourself the way God sees you. You may still be focused on outward appearance. You may be unhappy. You may be wondering if this is really what God had in mind when He created the beauty of male-female relationships.

It's not too late to take care of yourself. It's not too late to step back and deal with your hurt and your poor self-image. It's not too late to turn to God because of a bad relationship or a bad decision.

If you want to find the very best love for the rest of your life, you need to start with yourself. You need to learn to enjoy your own company before you expect anyone else to do that for you. You need to pray to God to help you heal your own wounds, and then you need to be willing to do the work that has to be done in order to make a lasting change.

You are a child of God. You are capable of a happy, healthy relationship and a happy, healthy self-image. Let's begin that process today.

WORKBOOK

Chapter One Questions

Question: Why is emotional health and wholeness so important before entering a relationship? What happens if one or both partners are looking to the other to meet their needs?

If you aren't whole as a single, you'll go into a relationship searching for fulfillment, which leads to broken hearts, damage, + disaster.

Question: What is the danger of dating someone who constantly wants to fix you or make you change?

You'll never experience the freedom of being loved for who you are as long as you're w/ them. It will cause you to remain insecure in the relationship + w/i yourself.

Question: What are ways that a person who has low self-esteem, a history of being abused, a history of bad relationships, or difficulty loving themselves can find healing before continuing the search for a mate?

Spend a season in God's presence + allow Him to heal those broken parts of you before inviting anyone into your life. Don't date until you establish your identity + contentment alone.

_Pray for healing +
do the work required_

Activity: Make a singleness "bucket list"—ideas for travel, ministry, volunteering, investments, learning, career building, and friendships that you can fully enjoy/be most dedicated to while still single. Then set goals to complete the items on your list and relax from focusing on finding a relationship.

_Obtain a purposeful career
Grow my business
Go to Beijing
Take a cruise
Start an asset portfolio
1 year of savings
Make more friends
Go to 1 concert a month
Double my salary
Become a better cook
Develop as a pro/bus owner
Get a new Audi Q5 +
paint it dark mauve blush w/ rose
gold accents_

Chapter One Notes

A healthy relationship =
2 ppl who are rooted in
PURPOSE + IDENTITY

Paris is still Paris if you
go by yourself!

Major key #1: value
yourself + your existence

Are you ready/willing to
give your ALL to someone
else, even when you feel
you have nothing left??

CHAPTER TWO

Shedding Shame

Instead of your shame ye shall have double; and instead of dishonor they shall rejoice in their portion: therefore in their land they shall possess double: everlasting joy shall be unto them.

—Isaiah 61:7

Sometimes on the road to getting to know ourselves and working on our self-image, we run into some bumps. Issues from the past come up and threaten to derail us altogether:

You should have taken that job.
You should have told that person how you felt.
You shouldn't have made that decision.
You shouldn't have gotten yourself into this situation.

These hindsight guilt trips hinder our confidence and fill us with discomfort and regret. And too often, these past actions or inactions prevent us from moving forward in relationships the way Christ intended.

We can't change the past. We can't erase the things we did (or didn't do) that contributed to our bad situation today. (We would need a time machine to do that!)

If, as you work on getting to know yourself and improve yourself, you feel trapped by your past mistakes and cornered by all those "I should haves and I shouldn't haves," then I have good news for you: God is not mad at you. He is not placing that feeling of shame upon your life. In fact, He wishes that you would shed that shame and live with your eyes facing forward, correcting the things that need to be corrected and leaving the past behind you.

Shame is one of the weapons that the devil uses to dismantle the lives of believers.

Poisoned by Shame

Shame knocks off your confidence, and as a result it affects your ability to succeed as men and women of God. But shame can do even more damage to your heart and soul. Shame will have you thinking that everybody around you knows about your past.

In my years of ministry and in countless conversations with believers, I have found that:

Shame punishes you. It makes you think you don't deserve another opportunity, because you've already ruined everything to the point of no return.

Shame paralyzes you, preventing you from moving forward. Even when you think you've moved on by leaving a marriage or a relationship, you take that shame from that relationship with you. It is guaranteed to pop up again in your life.

Shame makes you paranoid. You end up running from stuff that's not chasing you as you start to see and believe things that aren't there. This happened to Elijah in 1 Kings 19:2–4, when he ran into the wilderness, paranoid because of a message that he had misinterpreted from Jezebel. Elijah was so distraught that he even asked God to take his life! His shame had confused everything in his mind to the point that he wanted to die. Shame will have you running from nonexistent threats, too.

Shame distorts your thinking, and it opens your mind and your heart to psychological and spiritual warfare. Once the seed of shame is planted, the devil moves in. He makes you doubt truth and he whispers lies into your mind. He breaks down all trust that you once had in God, leaving you hopeless for a way out.

Shame is one of the greatest evils that the devil uses against believers. It poisons us from the inside out and affects every relationship, every opportunity, and every aspect of our being.

One Thing Leads to Another

Here's where it gets real: We all have done something in the past of which we are not proud. And because of this, we all are susceptible to shame. Every single one of us.

The thing in our past might something big, like breaking the law, or it might be less serious, such as saying something hurtful to someone. But whatever the offense, it can bring shame into our lives.

When Adam and Eve sinned by eating the fruit from the forbidden tree, they lost their God-consciousness and instead became self-conscious. They suddenly noticed their nakedness, and as a result they experienced shame (Genesis 3:8–12).

Adam and Eve are proof that shame exposes you. It strips away the glory of God, and it causes you to hide from the very Lord who has the power to change your predicament. Allowing shame to linger in your head and in your heart prevents you from getting over your sins, from leaving your past in the past, and from moving on with your life.

Steps to Overcome

Yes, shame messes with your head; it punishes you, paralyzes you, and makes you run away from things that don't even chase you. You find yourself hiding from the only One who can help you. But I am here to tell you that you don't have to spend the rest of your days living like that!

The Bible tells us, "Yea, none that wait for thee shall be put to shame" (Psalm 25:3). Jesus died for your sins and for your shame, and as a result: "Beloved, if our heart condemn us not, we have boldness toward God" (1 John 3:21). So, stop drowning yourself in all those negative emotions, mulling over past mistakes and worrying about what other people think of you and your sins. Living in shame is your decision, which means that dumping it is also your decision.

If you happen to be ashamed of your past, if your confidence has suffered because of what you feel you should or shouldn't have done, then this teaching is for you. I have put together four steps to tackle shame and stop ruining your life and your chance for happiness.

Make a conscious decision to overcome your shame. The first step is mental. Just as shame plays a mind game, you need to fight a mind battle against it. Make the conscious decision to shake off shame and never let it take over your mind and your heart again.

Ask God to free you from it. Once you have made the mental choice to overcome shame, let God deliver you from its grasp. Just as He freed you from sin, He can also free you from this guilt. Simply stand in His presence and ask: "In thee, O Jehovah, do I take refuge: let me never be put to shame: Deliver me in thy righteousness" (Psalm 31:1).

Guard yourself so it doesn't happen again. The Bible says to "gird your loins with truth" and to "put on the breastplate of righteousness" (Ephesians 6:14). If you want to be successful in life and in relationships, you need to accept the truth and make sure you do the right thing.

With your "breastplate of righteousness" on, you can't be willingly engaging in sinful behaviors while you ask

God to watch out for your kids. You can't tell God to handle your guilt while you make bad decision after bad decision. You have to desire to change your patterns and change your life! You have to strive to live as Christ has asked you to live.

Following God's advice and guarding yourself with truth and righteousness also means that you will become calmer and more at peace with yourself and the world. Your attitude will change. Your desires and outlook will change as God will keep you in check. By overcoming the shame of the past, you will have the power to leave your past behind and start living a truly blessed life.

Ditch the fake prosperity. This is a message aimed particularly at men: *Stop pretending that you are who you aren't.* Don't try to make yourself look richer, show off money that you don't have, or waste your hard-earned cash on worthless stuff you don't even need. Don't lie about how big your house is or how much you're earning. These untruths will set you on a path that will lead straight back to shame!

Instead, if you are interested in a woman, be honest with her. Let her know that you are still a work in progress, and that while you're still working toward that perfect job and better lifestyle, you want to get to know her better over coffee and quality time spent together.

If she is a woman worth pursuing, she'll appreciate your honesty, and you will continue to guard your heart against the poison of shame.

God Is the Antidote

As this chapter comes to a close, it's worth revisiting the scripture with which we began:

Instead of your shame ye shall have double; and instead of dishonor they shall rejoice in their portion: therefore in their land they shall possess double; everlasting joy shall be unto them.

—Isaiah 61:7

Shame is a ploy of the devil intended to break our trust in God and keep us so focused on the past that we are useless in the future.

If you have made mistakes in your past, if you have sinned, then come clean and ask God for help to set you free. Don't let shame and guilt linger in your life. It will mess with your head, and it will feed into the devil's psychological warfare against you.

Instead, follow the steps I've provided, and turn your life around for God and for that special someone who is out there waiting to have a healthy relationship with you. If you are open and honest, armed with truth and righteousness, then you will experience God's joy in your relationship.

WORKBOOK

Chapter Two Questions

Question: How does Satan use shame to cripple a believer from moving forward to a healthy future?

He uses it to make us paranoid, make us feel like we don't deserve better, make us enter into distorted thinking & spiritual warfare & to paralize us.

Questions: What mistakes, sins, inadequacies and/or failures in your past cause you shame? What things in your present do you find yourself trying to hide or lie about?

Money, promiscuity, fear, disobedience, my job, being nasty in building my business, the growth of my business

Question: In what areas do you need to choose obedience and set extra guards to protect yourself from sin and the shame that follows?

Operating in fear + insecurity, Lustful thoughts + behaviors + desires

_____

_____

_____

_____

_____

_____

Action: Write out a prayer to God acknowledging your shame, asking Him to free you from it, and committing yourself to His ways and His best for your future. Choose to live in authenticity toward God and others. Put your prayer in your Bible, journal, or another place where you can review it often when Satan tries to attack you with shame.

Heavenly Father,
I acknowledge my sin &
the shame associated w/
it. I ask you to free me
from the shame just as
you've freed me from my
sins. I commit myself to
your will + your ways.
I choose to live authen-
tically, completely shame
free. In Jesus' name, Amen.

Chapter Two Notes

Shame:
1) punishes you
2) paralizes you
3) makes you paranoid
4) distorts your thinking

1) Decide to overcome it
2) Ask God to free you
3) Guard yourself from it happening again

shame is used by the devil to break our trust in God + make us focus on the past so that we become useless in the future

CHAPTER THREE

Raising the Standards

When the adversary shall come I like a flood, the Spirit of Jehovah will lift up a standard...
—*Isaiah 59:19* *(ASV footnote)*

Some of us have been blessed by being raised in strong families by parents who provided a stellar example of a healthy, godly relationship. But most of us weren't as fortunate.

We come from broken homes in which Dad was absent and Mom worked two jobs. We come from abusive situations or neglectful situations. We come from hunger, alcohol, and disruption. When these are the themes of our past, how do we know what a healthy relationship even looks like? How can we possibly know what is good and what is bad?

Dysfunctional relationships are abundant in today's society, and they hurt the people involved very deeply. But how can you spot one before it happens to you? What are the signs? And how can you avoid them going forward?

It all starts with raising your standards.

Soul Ties

One type of problematic relationship comes as a result of an ungodly soul tie. A soul tie happens every time you link yourself with someone else. It happens when you decide to date *and* when you decide to be friends with someone. It also happens when you have sex and when you share intimacy with another person. Whenever you connect with someone else on any level, you pick up a part of their spirit, their nature—good or bad—and it stays with you. I call this a soul tie.

We've discussed the importance of learning to love and respect yourself. We've also discussed dealing with shame. These two steps are so very important, because if you don't deal with those issues first, you will find yourself jumping into a relationship that you think will fill that gap. It's a sort of surrogate relationship that is meant to make up for the fact that you don't like yourself, that you aren't comfortable in your own skin, and that you feel shame from the past.

It becomes a quick fix for your broken heart, and oftentimes it takes the shape of a one-night stand or a brief summer fling that will haunt you for the rest of your life. The more you seek out these relationships to fill the void inside of you, the more soul ties you will collect—evidence of meaningless relationships that should have never taken place to begin with.

While this approach doesn't typically involve abuse or manipulation, it does involve using people for selfish gain—over and over again. With any relationship that we get into, we must ask ourselves: Does this relationship exemplify a life of high standards? Do my motives line up with Christ's will for my life?

Dysfunction in the Church

Sadly, the church is not an exception to the prevalence of shallow one-night stands or toxic relationships. Over the past ten years, I've seen an increasing number of Christians whom I would call serial daters.

The truly scary thing, though, is that I've also seen an increasing number of Christians who are tied down by and trapped within truly dysfunctional relationships, both inside of and outside of marriage.

These differ from one-night stands in that these relationships are deeply rooted in manipulation and abuse. And they are very hard to change. The oppressor will never voluntarily change or grant the other person their freedom, and the oppressed will struggle to stand up for themselves and demand a better life—even though that is precisely what they need to do in order to find freedom. It is an endless cycle that can take years if not decades to break.

This is why it is crucial for all of us to learn how to spot a potentially dysfunctional partner, and then avoid or extricate ourselves from that connection completely.

Here are five symptoms of a dysfunctional relationship. Take a minute to see if any of these apply to whatever relationship you may be in today.

1. Physical abuse in any form. Physical abuse includes beating, pushing, slapping, or any form of physical contact that is intended to control or harm a person against their will. This is the most obvious evidence of a toxic relationship, and most people know how to spot it. However, many Christians neglect to do anything about it. They think that they have to put up with the abuse because of the vows they made to stick it out "for better, for worse, until death do us part." I am here to tell you, those vows do not give someone the liberty to physically hurt you. God *never* intended that marriage would be a cross for you to bear for the rest of your life.

2. Emotional or psychological abuse. Examples of this kind of abuse are undermining, bad-mouthing, putting the other person down, and gaslighting (which is manipulating the other person so that he/she doubts their own sanity). These forms of abuse are harder to spot, because the abuser is better at manipulating the situation and explaining his or her actions. Many times, the abused partner truly believes that they themselves are the problem. But the truth is that there is *no place* for any of these things in any relationship. A truly loving partner would *never* call you names, make you feel bad about yourself, or berate you.

3. Complete reliance on the other person. This can look like constant texting, complete financial reliance with no access to one's own funds, an inability to have fun with friends without the partner there, a need to know what the other is doing at all times, etc. It may seem strange to call a couple who cannot stand to be apart "dysfunctional," but that's exactly what they are. This type of dysfunction happens when one or both partners lack self-esteem and trust. They feel the need to control and are afraid by what may happen if they lose that control for even a little while. Remember, every relationship should be mutually beneficial, and there should be freedom for both parties to enjoy life.

4. Fear of the unknown. This dysfunction happens when one of the partners is in the relationship simply because they're afraid. They could be afraid of loneliness. They could be afraid of the isolation they might experience if they broke up and lost all of the friendships they had built while the relationship was going. They could be afraid of the shame they would feel if they chose not to get married despite the fact that they were pregnant.

Fear is a powerful motivator that can also lead to dysfunction. If you stay in a relationship because of fear rather than love for the other person, then you are missing out on a healthy relationship.

5. Tolerance of sin. In this situation, you may know he's sleeping around or that she's spending all your money on clothing or on drugs, and yet you can't bring yourself to leave. You don't want to face the shame of a failed relationship. You don't want everyone to see you as a victim. You don't want the pity. If you're married to the person, you know you need to challenge them and bring their actions out into the open, and yet you're paralyzed by the thought. Perhaps you've tried in the past and been shut down. Perhaps you have your own issues that could also be exposed in the process.

Sin in any relationship is complete dysfunction, and it will only pull you further away from a complete, healthy relationship until you begin to address the issue and work through it.

Living with the Devil

Even if you can spot a dysfunctional person or relationship from a mile away, how do you deal with it? How can you really turn dysfunction around?

Dysfunctional relationships will never correct themselves. The only way to move toward healing is to demand change. It's up to the victim to demand that they be treated better. It's up to the controlled to demand their freedom.

Be warned of empty words, though. I have met many abused women (although I have seen men who are abuse victims, as well) who have told me, "He beats me up, Pastor, but then he comes back with a tear in his eye and says that he loves me so much and that he is sorry. Then he promises this will never happen again. In that moment I ask for change, and he agrees. But then the cycle starts all over again. What am I supposed to do?"

My response is simple. People who are truly repentant should always be given another chance. Let him seek help. Let him work though his issues. But you do not need to stay in the same house with him while he does this. Safety is imperative in these situations.

It Starts with Standards

All of this—one-night stands, brief flings, extreme dysfunction, and abuse—can be avoided when we learn to spot the signs. But we will only find true happiness when we also demand higher standards for ourselves and for our relationships.

I've seen many couples who are together simply because their marriage is good enough to endure. There's no abuse. There's no dysfunction. But I'm here to tell you there isn't anything to enjoy, either!

To truly find joy in your union, you have to set a high standard. You have to put your trust in God and live according to His law. You have to "gird your loins with truth and put on the breastplate of righteousness" (Ephesians 6:14). Don't be like Adam and Eve who allowed sin to enter into their relationship by eating of the forbidden tree and then hiding from God (Genesis 3:6). Don't get into relationships that are not of God. Set a high standard for yourself. *Demand better!*

WORKBOOK

Chapter Three Questions

Question: What are soul ties and why are they dangerous?
Have you ever used a temporary relationship to hide from
the loneliness and pain in your heart?

- Soul Ties = picking up
  a part of someone's
  spirit + nature by
  connecting w/ them

- You could be picking
  up the wrong spirit

- Definitely

Question: Describe characteristics of a dysfunctional relationship. How can you safeguard yourself from physical or emotionally abusive relationship? When does dependence on the other person cross the line to being unhealthy co-dependence?

- Abuse, co-dependence, fear, tolerating sin.

- Raise your standards

- When you can't be apart, when you become controlling & fearful of being without them

Question: How should a Christian respond to abuse in a relationship? What is a healthy way to "give another chance" or show forgiveness?

Forgive, give another chance, but do so from a distance as they seek help to change

_____

_____

_____

_____

_____

_____

_____

_____

Action: Are you ready to raise the standard? Consider the marriages that you have seen modeled within your family, friends, and church. Are they healthy or dysfunctional? Write down a description of the type of God-honoring marriage you want to have. Invite people in your life to help keep you accountable if you appear to be in a toxic relationship.

A representation of God's love
faithful
forgiving
supportive
affectionate
open communication
fun
committed completely
unbreakable

Chapter Three Notes

_____

_____

_____

_____

_____

_____

_____

_____

_____

_____

_____

_____

_____

_____

_____

_____

_____

_____

_____

CHAPTER FOUR

Prepare to Be Picky

And it came to pass in the morning that, behold, it was Leah: and he said to Laban, What is this thou hast done unto me? Did not I serve with thee for Rachel?
—Genesis 29:25.

Have you ever woken up and realized that the person who was sleeping next to you was not the right person for you? Literally or figuratively, whether your discovery was made after a one-night stand in bed or during a dinner out, you may have experienced that moment in which it dawns on you that the person you're with isn't the one you want to be with.

This kind of a situation happened to Jacob, who, after serving seven years to get Rachel as his wife, found himself waking up next to Leah.

And Jacob loved Rachel; and he said, I will serve thee

seven years for Rachel thy younger daughter. And Laban said, It is better that I give her to thee, than that I should give her to another man: abide with me. And Jacob served seven years for Rachel; and they seemed unto him but a few days, for the love he had to her.

And Jacob said unto Laban, Give me my wife, for my days are fulfilled, that I may go in unto her. And Laban gathered together all the men of the place, and made a feast. And it came to pass in the evening, that he took Leah his daughter, and brought her to him; and he went in unto her. And Laban gave Zilpah his handmaid unto his daughter Leah for a handmaid. And it came to pass in the morning that, behold, it was Leah: and he said to Laban, What is this thou hast done unto me? did not I serve with thee for Rachel? wherefore then hast thou beguiled me?
—Genesis 29:18-25

In Jacob's circumstance, the mix-up wasn't entirely his fault. He had been promised Rachel as his wife, and yet he'd been given Leah. When he discovered what had happened, he argued against it and then took steps to make Rachel his wife, as well.

But so often in today's culture, we may start out with a Leah and not do anything to change the situation. Or we may chase after a Leah even though we know we'd be happier with a Rachel.

Now, let me clarify what I mean by a "Leah" and a "Rachel." I'm not advocating jumping from person to person, chasing after your ever-changing emotions. I am talking about having a standard.

I am using this example of Leah and Rachel as a metaphor. Rachel represents someone with whom you are equally yoked—compatible—and with whom you can pursue God in your relationship.

Leah, on the other hand, represents a toxic relationship: when you are with this person, you become a worse version of yourself. Together you draw each other away from God and from what matters.

We live in a time when the songs, movies, TV programs, and books to which we are exposed almost seem to promote a life of promiscuity. These relationships create a complex network of soul ties that we can't easily shake off or move on from. We waste valuable time when we pursue Leah's—and we put a lot on the line. A causal relationship will produce lifelong consequences when a child is born, or when one's identity quickly becomes entangled with another's identity.

But when your choice is right—when you hold out for that Rachel—then your life will be right, as well.

Put in the Time

Think about how many hours of hard work and learning it takes to get a driver's license. You take a class, commit to some hands-on training, and are required to take numerous tests. Only after you pass everything are you permitted to drive—and rightly so. Driving is a dangerous activity for those who are unprepared and uneducated.

Marriage can also be a dangerous thing to jump into—and yet you can get married on a whim for less than a family dinner will cost you. There are places where you can tie the knot at a drive-through! Today's society has tried to cheapen the value of marriage, seemingly forgetting that God created a man, then He created a woman, and then He brought them together in the institution of marriage.

As God's Word warns, "Be not deceived; God is not mocked: for whatsoever a man soweth, that shall he also reap" (Galatians 6:7). If you marry someone at a drive-through, you're taking the risk that your marriage will be nothing more than a fast-food meal. It may fill your stomach at the moment of hunger, but it's not a healthy choice, nor is it going to nourish you in the long run.

To prepare for marriage and to find the right person for you, you have to be willing to invest time and effort.

Get a Job, Brother!

Did you read this heading and think: *Whoa, Pastor, aren't you being a bit too harsh?* I'm sorry if you did, but truth can be harsh! Part of investing effort means choosing to be a responsible adult and earn a living.

When God created Adam, "[He] took the man, and put him into the garden of Eden to dress it and to keep it" (Genesis 2:15). That's right—God gave Adam a job before He gave him a wife, and when He provided the wife, it was with the statement that it wasn't good for the man to be handling all of the responsibilities by himself.

Think about that. *Because* man had all of those responsibilities, God wanted him to have a helper. A man who doesn't work probably doesn't need a spouse!

Now, I'm not talking about those men who lose a job out of no fault of their own. I'm talking about the guys who don't even try to get a job. The men who have no ambition or drive or sense of responsibility whatsoever.

Even though in the modern world today, women often work to help make ends meet, God's will is for the man to be the giver and the supplier while a woman's job was to take that provision and make it better. That was the original plan, and I believe strongly that when we settle for less, we are settling for Leah.

Another truth that I believe is that men should never be uptight about having to provide for their families, because if they're with the right woman, then she'll never take advantage of the situation. A real woman—the *right* woman—will take what you bring her and make it more, better, happier. This is God's ultimate plan for marriage.

Garbage In, Garbage Out

Another issue I see in today's "quick" marriages comes when spouses complain that their needs aren't being met. I hear this a lot, actually—and fair enough. When our needs are not being met, we do get grumpy, don't we? We become unhappy.

But as I said before, every relationship should be mutually beneficial. So when, in the midst of our "fast food" marriages, we find that our needs aren't being met, are we taking a moment and asking ourselves if we are fulfilling our spouse's needs? Are we giving freely in addition to expecting to receive as freely?

A man provides for his family, and a woman takes it and gives it back in an even greater measure. You give her groceries; she'll give you a meal. You give her a house; she'll make it your home. You give her a seed; she'll give you a baby. But be careful! You give her hell; she'll run you out.

This principle can be extended to your life in general: If you don't put in loving deeds, don't expect happiness or contentment in return.

Jacob is an example of someone who fell victim to this simple principle. He played everybody, manipulated his parents, stole his brother's birthright (Genesis 25)—and guess what? Laban played him out by giving him the wrong woman for a wife.

Dating Done Right

We've talked about how to avoid the wrong people and how to buck up and accept responsibility, but how and where do you find that Mr. or Miss Right?

Over the years of working with people, helping them build better relationships and blessed marriages, I have realized that you only need to follow a few powerful principles to find the right person for you. Dating is not a recreational activity, but an important time to prepare for the rest of your life. If you understand that and are prepared to make a real connection and the work that should precede a commitment to someone in marriage, keep reading. Below are the four rules for dating that will help you build a loving, caring, God-blessed marriage:

1. Both parties must be saved. This is a fundamental message for Christians, but it can be extended to anyone who lives by godly principles: "Be not unequally yoked with unbelievers: for what fellowship have righteousness and iniquity? Or what communion hath light with darkness?" (2 Corinthians 6:14). If you have principles, make sure the other party shares them. If you are a Christian, you should want your significant other to be one, too. You want your spouse to believe in and share the same fundamental beliefs.

2. Men who seek weak women aren't worth it. This message is for you, ladies. Don't bother getting involved with someone who is not at your level. Don't waste your life with a guy who is intimidated by your strength and/or lacking in self-esteem. And certainly don't wait for them to develop in these areas! If you yourself are strong, then you need a match who complements that strength. You need to find a mate who will match you and bring the best out in you, but don't go too overboard. Seek to be a helpmate, but don't seek *for* a helpmate.

3. Never make emotional decisions when it comes to relationships. I see this every day in my pastoral practice. A couple comes in saying, "Pastor, we want to get married, because we love each other." And I reply: "That's great, but how can you be sure it's the real thing, and not just the pizza you ate last night?"

Yes, this example is a bit tongue-in-cheek, but the real message is as serious as it gets with marriage. Going back to the biblical definitions of "love," it's important to know whether you love someone the way you love ice cream or a one-night-stand, or whether you love someone with a deep, everlasting *agape* kind of love.

Agape is what you want in marriage. *Agape* love treats

the other person right because there are no expectations to get something in return, and there's no exchange of favors. *Agape* love is when you love the person at their best and at their worst. It's unconditional, regardless of what you ate last night or of how good this person made you feel this morning.

Emotions come and go; they change with the wind. But *agape* love lasts. You should never make important decisions based on the fickleness emotions, but on the bedrock of *agape* love.

4. Don't waste your life on someone who has no commitment level. I've said this before in many different ways, but I'll do it again: Because we only have one life here on earth, don't waste it on someone who is not ready to commit to the marriage you want to have. As soon as you realize that your significant other is only interested in having fun, walk away. There are far too many other people in the world to wait for this person to "get ready" or to spend time worrying about the situation. Just walk. Walk away.

Be Picky

If you don't want to be like Jacob, waking up with the wrong woman, then don't be a player. Don't waste time on "having fun." Instead, use the time you have wisely, following God's principles. Look for the right person and look in the right places. Learn to recognize when a person is not right for you and have the courage to walk away from those relationships.

Raise your standard. Get back to the Bible and make up your mind that if you are going to have a relationship, it will be the one that God designed for you to have. Sure, we live in an age in which people usually partner up without a second thought. They have babies with multiple partners, and they move in together at the drop of a hat. You don't have to perpetuate the cycle. Be picky. Be aware of players. And prepare yourself to be the man or woman you need to be in order to find your Rachel.

WORKBOOK

Chapter Four Questions

Question: Describe a time when you were dating someone and realized they were the wrong person for you. What helped you to realize they were not a good fit for you to partner your life with?

I realized they weren't right for me when the relationship made me feel worse about myself & further away from God.

Question: Why is it important for a man to have a job before he finds a wife? How does the right woman complement a man's loving provision for the family?

- Because she can't be a help meet to you if you aren't bringing anything to the table

- She takes it a multiplies it. She turns groceries into a meal, a house into a home, a seed into a child.

Question: What is the difference between recreational dating and dating to find a spouse? How do you know if the person you are dating is marriage material?

- Dating for fun vs. dating with a purpose in mind.

- They are willing to invest time + effort

_____

_____

_____

_____

_____

_____

Action: Define and describe your "Rachel." What are the qualities you seek in a mate? Make a list of those things that are essential for you. Commit yourself to waiting for God's best.

- Lives for God, has an intimate rel. w/ Him + a strong prayer life
- A man of vision, has a plan for his life + is working towards it
- Patient
- willing to communicate
- Affectionate (intentionally)
- Intelligent
- Protector (phys, emo, spirit, ment)
- Hilarious + Fun
- Smooth + full of swag
- Has a pure heart + compassion for others
- Supportive
- Financially stable + literate

Chapter 4 Notes

CHAPTER FIVE

Stay United

Beloved, let us love one another: for love is of God; and
every one that loveth is begotten of God, and knoweth God
—1 John 4:7

There is a metaphor I love that talks about the differences between men and women. It says that women are like oranges. Their beauty is obvious from the outside, but the inside is also full of nutrients. To get to the juicy inside, you have to peel back the layers. And once you're there, you soon notice the various sections—the various aspects of her personality. Before you can enjoy the full benefits of this relationship, you have to get to know these sections intimately.

Men, on the other hand, are like apples. There are no sections; what you get is what you see. Apples are good for you; they are healthy and delicious. But apples bruise easily. What's more, you can't spot those bruises very easily—men are good at hiding their bruises, even pretending there aren't any. A man may look strong, but that doesn't mean he hasn't been bruised by life. What's more, a man's bruises don't necessarily spoil the fruit. You can cut them out and still enjoy the apple.

What this tells me is that before you can enjoy the full benefits of a relationship with a woman, you have to get to know the aspects of her personality intimately. And to enjoy the full benefits of a relationship with a man, you must understand that even though a man may have been hurt by life, that doesn't mean that he should be tossed aside.

The most beautiful thing about men and woman and my fruity metaphor is that both oranges and apples have seeds inside. And the role of these seeds is to plant, to start all over. It means that no matter how much damage you have suffered, if God is on your side, then He gives you another chance to start over again.

A Collision of Histories

We've talked about getting yourself ready to find the right person, but that's just the beginning, because once you find that special someone, then you have even more work to do. You need to prepare yourselves for marriage.

If it hadn't been for the work my wife and I have put into and continue to put into our marriage, we wouldn't be where we are today. Marriage is ongoing work. You start working on it the moment you know the person you are dating is the "right one," and you keep working on it until death do you part.

This is because marriage is hard. It's not a simple coming together of two people; it's a collision of two worlds and two histories.

Marriage is like taking an airline flight: You've got a destination to reach, you have a starting point, you both need to get on the same plane, you both need a ticket (your marriage license), you get on the plane excited, and there is smooth cruising and bumpy parts. But in order to even take off and leave the ground, you need to limit your baggage. If you bring too much on board—with too many soul ties, too many sins, too much shame, and too many emotional and spiritual battles—it'll be too hard to truly get off the ground. And instead of landing in some beautiful place, you'll end up circling around the tarmac and never leave the home port.

Everyone brings baggage into a marriage. You come to the relationship with your own personality, your quirks, your sense of humor—even your train collection or your weakness for ice cream. But you also bring your less-than-perfect family and all sorts of emotional issues from your past. It's a lot—and just think: Your significant other brings the same amount of stuff into the marriage, if not more. Sometimes they bring children or other responsibilities, too.

This collision of two histories needs to be handled with care; it will need ongoing work.

The only way to guarantee that your marriage has a shot is to bind it with *agape* love. This love can't be based on a feeling of the moment, however fantastic it may seem.

If you want your marriage to be blessed with God's love, with *agape* love, you need to first understand what kinds of things He blesses, and then you must strive to follow those principles. If you make God the source of your relationship, this will cause the ongoing work on your marriage to be easier, because God is love, and love comes from Him (1 John 4:7).

Understand Their Side

The Bible says: "Ye husbands, in like manner, dwell with your wives according to knowledge, giving honor unto the woman, as unto the weaker vessel, as being also joint-heirs of the grace of life" (1 Peter 3:7). This is a very powerful principle for successful marital bliss, and for happiness in any other relationship: Understand how the other person functions, how he/she thinks, what makes her/him happy or sad, how he/she relates to people and the world around them.

Understanding comes with knowledge, and knowledge is a result of due diligence—of putting the effort and time into getting to know the other person. That's why the dating period is important. It's the time you need to spend with your partner in mutual exploration of the worlds and histories that you both are bringing to this relationship. During this time, you can talk about beliefs and principles. You can talk about moral values and dreams. But don't stop there.

Talk about little things, too—the things that form the fabric of our lives. Is he messy? Does she like to sleep in on Sundays? And most importantly: Can you live with those things?

Don't Push Change

Have you ever seen or heard someone say, "Oh, he might be like that now, but once we're married, he'll change"? Or they may say, "My love will change her, I'm sure." These are risky things to say! These people don't really get what makes a good relationship.

A good relationship that comes from God entails the acceptance of the person the way he/she is. A good relationship doesn't insist on changing the other person. Sure, there may be things that irritate us about our husband or wife, but a good marriage understands that those things probably won't change. And a good marriage is okay with that.

Just as you should believe yourself to be the child of God, beautiful and good, you should believe the same for the other person. Either this person is right for you and you can discuss your differences and arrive at a consensus and work through difficulties together, or the person is wrong for you and you will never be able to truly work through your obstacles.

Practice Mutual Authority

This is where many people get it wrong about Christian marriages. In the Bible, God said to Eve "thy desire shall be to thy husband, and he shall rule over thee" (Genesis 3:16).

Some people take this statement out of context. But I am here to tell you that just because you are married, that does not mean that someone can beat you up. God has never said that you should put yourself and your children in harm's way for the sake of a marriage. That is *not* what this verse is saying.

These words were pronounced by God after Adam and Eve sinned, which means that this setup was not part of God's original design. God's original plan was for husbands and wives to live their lives with God's blessing, and to "be fruitful, and multiply, and replenish the earth, and subdue it" (Genesis 1:28). This plan was for both man and woman equally.

God has given you, both husbands and wives, mutual authority. He did not mean for the man to rule over the woman, but for a woman and a man to submit one to another and to take on different roles—different jobs—within the marriage.

A man's role is to provide, and a woman's role is to take that provision and make it better. And let me clarify this, as this issue often comes up and becomes a source of many arguments. I believe women have their place in every arena of life, every sector of leadership, from the presidency to the ministry pulpits, to wherever else they are needed. And I think men need to be careful.

The fact that your wife earns five times more than you do doesn't take the responsibility of provision from you. You still have to provide. You still have to contribute. God gave you a job before He gave you a wife, remember? The man's role is to be the foundation, the platform on which the house is built, while the women are to take that house and create a home. So, even in today's culture I believe it's still very important for the man to be able to provide and for the woman to be able to create.

Beware of Attack

All of this may sound simple when you're reading it in a book, but it's hard to put into practice! The reason it's so hard to make a marriage work is that the devil gets involved. The devil doesn't want you to live in harmony, and he pulls his dirty tricks because he understands that the place of agreement is the place of power. If you and your spouse are united, then he stands little chance for victory. But if he can bring division between you, then he can slowly tear your relationship apart.

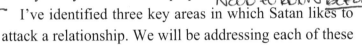
what don't understand out
need to know before marriage!

I've identified three key areas in which Satan likes to attack a relationship. We will be addressing each of these later on in this book.

1. Parenting. I have met many young couples who were doing really well together until they had their first child. Then, with the stress and joy of being a parent came a wave of arguments over what should be done and how with little Johnny. This is why it's imperative to have these conversations before you get married. You don't want to realize that you have two completely different parenting styles *after* you've welcomed your new little bundle of joy.

2. Sex and intimacy. When it comes to this area, men and women are different. Men are like microwaves: You drop your food on a paper plate, put it in, push the button, and *ding!* It's hot and ready. Women are more like Crock-Pots: You start it in the morning, put in the veggies, then potatoes, then add your meat, season it, leave it to simmer (preferably for hours), and after a slow, careful process, it's tender and full of flavor.

These differences can prove to be a huge hurdle in most marriages, which is why it's important to learn the art of negotiation—of giving and taking and coming to a consensus.

3. Money and finances. All those financial worries, all those unpaid bills, all those why-did-you-buy-this moments—this is all Satan's work to weasel his way into your marriage and break down your united front. Money and finances is a huge area that you need to learn to manage together before the devil gets a foothold.

A New Life

God created marriage as something for us to enjoy, not just tolerate. But it's important to keep in mind that marriage is nothing like dating. Marriage is day-in, day-out life with another person. He'll see you in the morning without your makeup, and she'll see you after a stressful day at work, when all you might want to do is veg out. You won't be able to just walk away from arguments, and you certainly won't be able to ignore the phone calls from each other when you're feeling angry.

Marriage is about learning to coexist peacefully—even when everything in you might want to take the day off.

But once you do learn to coexist—once you figure out

how to work together as a team and communicate properly—then marriage offers an incredible support system you can't get anywhere else.

God wants your relationship to be good enough to bring many years of happiness, comfort, stability, and support. He wants to bless you; He's rooting for you. But you must also do your part and pave the way for a united, mutually responsible marriage.

Getting to know to the other person and understanding how she or he functions is key preparation for this kind of marriage. Moreover, recognizing the three areas of attack the devil will try to bring and staying united against them is what will prevent the enemy from picking apart your relationship.

WORKBOOK

Chapter Five Questions

Question: How is every marriage impacted by a "collision of histories"? What history / baggage do you or will you bring to a relationship?

- Each is a product of their life experiences thus far t will be merging all of that together.

- Perfectionist
Overthinker
Overly independent
fear of ~~having~~ having a marriage like ~~my parents~~ my parents
Pride

Question: Do you seek to understand your partner or to change your partner? How can you grow in understanding? How can you work through differences?

- knowing that there may be things about you that they don't like as well

- Ask yourself if what's lacking or "wrong" is a bigger deal than the value they do bring to your life

- Be honest & communicate those things. They may be willing to consider what's bothering you

Question: Explain the principle of mutual authority. What is the role and responsibility of the husband? What is the role and responsibility of the wife?

- submitting to each other & being willing to take on diff. roles

- husband is to provide & wife's role is to take that provision & make it better

_____

_____

_____

_____

_____

_____

Action: It's time to talk. Look at the big three areas of marital attack—parenting, sex, and finances. If you are in a dating relationship, set aside at least one evening to talk through each of these areas. Have questions prepared ahead of time about each topic (many lists are available online or through Christian books). More will be discussed about each of these specific topics in the next three chapters.

If you are not in a dating relationship, think through your own beliefs about each of these topics. Review the list that you created for qualities to look for in a spouse. Did you include qualities that will help you be united in these three key areas?

Chapter Five Notes

CHAPTER SIX

Live Holy…
Even When You're Tempted

Meats for the belly, and the belly for meats: but God shall bring to nought both it and them. But the body is not for fornication, but for the Lord; and the Lord for the body.
—*1 Corinthians 6:13*

Let's talk about how to live holy when you're horny.

Did you flinch? Did you shake your head when you read that sentence? Or maybe you sighed with relief, thinking: *At last, someone who talks about it openly!*

I hope you're in the last group—I hope you recognize the need to talk openly about this topic.

Sexual desires are natural, and in our modern world, it is very difficult to be a single Christian living with sexual desires. The church doesn't do much to help—everyone acts like it isn't a problem, that there isn't lust and sex and desire going on within the congregation. The way I see it, there is no point in denying that we all experience these struggles of the flesh.

But more importantly, God can never deliver any of us from something that we won't even admit exists!

If you want to live according to God's principles, the first step is to be honest with yourself and God about the difficulties you are experiencing. Once you've done that, keep reading; I have some practical advice for you on how to live your life the way the Lord wants you to live when you're battling with sexual desire.

Sex Is Like a Fire

Sex is an important part of marriage, but it's also like a fire—warm and comforting when it's in the fireplace, but destructive if it's brought outside of it.

A God-blessed marriage is your safe fireplace, and within these confines, physical intimacy can bring you together. It creates a bond, and, of course, we also know that it enables you to have children.

When you allow yourself to become sexually active when you're not married, you open the door to a destructive force that can affect not only your present, but also your future. Sex outside of marriage brings soul ties with it. It creates intense connections with whomever you engage in it, and it introduces the possibility of children, which become forever physical ties to that person.

The Bible says: "Therefore shall a man leave his father and his mother, and shall cleave unto his wife: and they shall be one flesh" (Genesis 2:24). The message here is straightforward: God only meant for us to have a sexual experience with one partner and in the context of marriage. God's original intent was for both people to be virgins before they joined in the union.

But what if you don't fit this bill? What if you happened to consummate your relationship before your wedding day? Yes, you missed the mark, but it's not all lost! Jesus died for situations such as this, and it's never too late to begin living right again through the Holy Spirit.

Desire Is Natural

God created us to have sexual desire. He knew exactly what He was doing when He formed our bodies the way He did, and when He placed within us a desire for intimacy. So yes, it's normal to feel horny!

If you've ever prayed, "Lord, just take that desire away from me," you might have gotten yourself into trouble. On the one hand, you're asking God to help you find the right person to marry, but on the other hand, you're asking God to shut off something that your body greatly needs—something that God intended for you to have!

Now, how should God respond to a prayer like that? What if He took away the desire permanently? I don't think any of us really wants that to happen. What we want is a way to deal with and handle our desires in the way that Christ would have us deal with and handle them. The point is not to cut sexual desire out of your life, but to be able to control it in a God-honoring way.

The desire of the flesh is one of the most difficult things to manage. It's something that can defeat you easily, and if that happens, you will spend the rest of your life serving it. The results can be catastrophic.

I believe David's fight with Goliath is an incredible metaphor for our fight with our physical flesh (1 Samuel 17). He was Goliath, the tallest man anyone had ever seen. Strong, fierce, and powerful. And then you had David, a shepherd boy who was pretty good with a sling, but he was no warrior.

Yet David did not want Goliath to control him or his people. And so he stepped out and said to Goliath, "If you defeat me, we will serve you but I defeat you, you will serve us." This is how we should also deal with the flesh. We should be vigilant in gaining victory over it so that it may serve our needs, and not the other way around.

God has the power to help us through our desire. Through Him we can conquer our bodies and be the ones who are in control of our desires. This doesn't mean shutting them down entirely, but rather learning self-control in a way that enables us to wait for a perfect, God-blessed union.

Three Areas That Need Control

The Bible tells us to "walk by the Spirit, and ye shall not fulfil the lust of the flesh" (Galatians 5:16). The gist of self-control is to bring yourself under the guidance of the Holy Spirit. This takes discipline and wisdom, but it is doable with God's help.

Below are my top practical tips on staying in control of your body.

1. Know the power of music. We live in a society saturated with sex: advertising, movies, video games, music—everything is laced with sexual connotations. In my opinion, however, music is Satan's favorite modus operandi. Just look at all those lyrics filled with filth! And they aren't only sexual; there are God-defying lyrics, violent lyrics, and more. Music videos and live performances just seem to make it worse. Immodest movements, the lack of appropriate clothing—it's all just so focused on the flesh. If you want to control your lust, monitor the type of music you choose to listen to and the performances that you watch.

2. Keep your dates public. You can't live your life holy when you choose to go over to her house at 10 p.m. on a Friday night. That's a recipe for disaster. Instead, be realistic. How hard will it be to keep your meeting decent? Will you be able to respect each other and God if you're alone together at night?

Choosing to meet up in public or with friends is a great way to ensure that you don't put yourself in a compromising situation.

My mother taught me another trick that I still share with others, because I think it is a huge help. Growing up, every time we went shopping together, she instructed me not to nag her to buy me things and to keep my hands in my pockets, so I wouldn't be tempted to grab the toys she wasn't going to buy me.

"Don't touch anything you haven't paid for, John," she would say, and I think those words can be applied to sexual situations, as well. Ladies, every time someone asks you out, make it clear from the very beginning that you don't approve of physical intimacy before marriage. You're happy to go out and do something nice together but be up front that you want to avoid dark places, such as movie theaters. And men, remember that you have no right to touch anything you haven't paid for. Not only that, but you also have no right to nag her about it! Respect each other and respect the situation.

3. Real love will wait. As a Christian, you want to live up to God's standard. You want to be free to be yourself and walk in righteousness without being pressured to sin. If your boyfriend/girlfriend or fiancé/ fiancée is telling you, "Come on, it's been four months now, it's time to get physical," don't listen. Don't let him or her bully or trick you into thinking, "*If you love me, you will let me.*"

God's standard is, "*If you love me, you will wait.*"

The Bible says that "love suffereth long, and is kind" (1 Corinthians 13:4). Real love can wait, and it *will* wait because real love is kind. It doesn't pressure. It doesn't set forth ultimatums. It waits. It is patient. When someone is willing to wait until the time is right, then you know that he or she really loves you.

Waiting is hard, I know. I've been there. For seven years before I met my wife, I prayed that God would help me restrain my flesh. Seven years, day in and day out. This became a way of living for me. It was my reality for a very long time, and yet I'm living proof that God is able to help you control your desire when it needs to be controlled. He will keep you from sinning with your flesh if you just ask Him for help and if you rely on Him and keep Him part of the conversation.

It's not magic, though. He doesn't just show up randomly. You have to want His help, and He will deliver.

The Lust Problem

When I talk to young people who are preparing for marriage, they often ask me about resisting all temptations—because adultery isn't just the act of sleeping with someone. It can also include lust or even emotional affairs.

The Bible says, "Each man is tempted, when he is drawn away by his own lust, and enticed" (James 1:14). But the Bible is also very clear that: "Thou shalt not commit adultery" (Matthew 5:27).

So, while adultery can come in many forms, God still wants us to steer clear, no matter how "innocent" or "no big deal" a situation may seem. We must consider the desires of our heart *and* our head. Lust is one of the enemies that is weakening the greatest fibers of our society: our families.

Lust is a liar. You may have a beautiful wife or a handsome husband at home, but lust will tell you that that's not enough. It'll tell you that you "deserve more." It will convince you that there are better options out there, and that one fling, one emotional affair, one text exchange with another person, is what you need to get through. Lust is underhanded, because it never is truly satisfied.

Lust is sneaky, too. It comes in when you're in the room with your spouse, when you're being intimate and yet you're thinking of someone else. Lust comes in when you spend too much time looking at the opposite sex on Instagram. Lust convinces you that fun and beauty are happening elsewhere, and that you need to make some kind of change in your life (that is, find a new person or a new setting) to really experience it.

Lust can happen in your head, too. It can be a fantasy on which you continually dwell, or images that you've tucked away in your mind to think about later.

I am here to tell you it's not worth it. The thrill of someone new, the fantasy of what-could-be, will never give you true happiness. These things will never nurture your soul.

Manage Your Lust

Fortunately, God's Word provides solutions to avoid the damage brought on by unbridled sexual desire. God made us thinking creatures. He gave us a free will and the ability to exercise self-control. This is your best weapon in the warfare with lust, so use it! Here are a few tips on managing your lust:

Beware of advertisements. It is estimated that in America, each individual sees up to ten thousand brand messages per day.[2] And you know that these little devils are laced with sexual connotations. Make it easier for yourself: Stop watching television commercials, turn your attention off when you hear them on the radio, learn to ignore ads in the press, limit your time on the Internet, and install ad-blocking software if you need to.

Say "no" to pornography. This rule may sound obvious, but every second, 372 people are typing the word "adult"—as in *adult content*—into their search engines. Forty million Americans visit porn sites regularly, and about 30 percent of these visitors are women.[3] I promise you, it will be easier to manage your lust if you avoid pornography completely.

Get a dumb phone. We live in a world where you can have access the web and all its resources at all times, thanks to your smartphone. But if your phone tempts you to visit ungodly sites, to look at lust-fueling photos, or to have arousing chats with strangers, then get rid of it. Get a dumb phone.

You've Got This!

If I could do it, you can do it, too. I've known many people who have been successful inn living a lust-free life, because they knew how to live holy when they were horny. The key is to remember that your body craves sex, just like your belly craves meat. There's nothing wrong with this; it's completely normal and natural. But your body is also a member of Christ; don't make it a member of a harlot (1 Corinthians 6:15).

Yes, the devil will come to tempt you. He will whisper that "you deserve this" into your ear, and he will do everything he can to make you believe that it is worth it. That you are powerless against the lusts of the flesh in your body.

But you *can* resist. You have the ability to resist and

the power to resist, because you are a child of God. Pray to the Lord and He will help you bring your lust and desire under the control of the Holy Spirit. He has the power to not only deliver you from all the sins of your flesh, but also to keep you living right. Trust Him and follow His principles. As 1 Corinthians 6:13 says, "[The body] is for the Lord; and the Lord for the body."

WORKBOOK

Chapter Six Questions

Question: Since sexual desire is natural, is it possible to bring it under the Holy Spirit's control? How?

Yes, be careful + inten-
tional about what you
watch + listen to. Create
boundaries when dating.
Pray + ask God to help
you contain your urges
in a God-honoring way

Question: What are leading causes of sexual temptation in the culture today? What are practical steps that you can take to avoid sexual sin?

Music, ads, performances. Block ads, get a dumb phone, no porn

Question: "Lust is a liar." What are some of the lies that lust whispers to your heart, and what is God's truth that can overcome those lies?

That you can't control it, that you're missing out on something, that you deserve it.

God's given us the free
Will + ability to use
self-control

Action: Try a social media/internet/tv fast for one week. Does time away from these reduce your temptations toward lust and sexual sin? Are there things you need to permanently cut out of your life? Are there safeguards you can put in place for the things that remain?

Chapter Six Notes

CHAPTER SEVEN

Master Your Money

For which of you, desiring to build a tower, doth not first sit down and count the cost, whether he have wherewith to complete it?

—*Luke 14:28*

Do you know what is one of the most common reasons that marriages, even Christian ones, fail? Money. Yes, good ol' money. It's a problem when you don't have enough; it's a problem when you always want more; and it's a problem when you disagree on how to manage it.

Money certainly makes the world go 'round, and it can make even the most in-love couple split apart in hurtful ways. I've seen that happen many times in my marital guidance practice, because Christians are in no way exempt from allowing money issues to creep into their marriages.

Just as with many other potential hot spots in marriage, being open about money and talking through financial issues during the early stages in your relationship can help you manage your marriage better, even in the midst of financial difficulty.

Start with an Agreement

Not every divorce that is filed due to financial conflicts is caused by poverty or a lost job. Many times, financial disagreements come down to simple differences in how each person approaches money management. There are different views on how to handle bills, how much to spend, how much to save, and what to do with anything that may be left over.

Amos 3:3 asks, "Shall two walk together, except they have agreed?" And this is the key to your marital financial bliss: You have to have a joint attitude to money. Even if you differ at the beginning, you have to talk about it, iron these issues out, and decide on a joint approach *before* you tie the knot. And if you can't see yourself ever coming into agreement on your financial perspectives, then you may need to reconsider the relationship. Money is guaranteed to be a point of stress until an agreement is reached.

Below are some key aspects of financial management you should discuss with your fiancé or fiancée.

Don't Ignore Debt

Financial problems are very common in modern-day America, and the older we get, the more debt we typically carry. The statistics are overwhelming: The average American household is carrying $15,983 in credit card debt, and \$133,568 in overall debt.[4] We are living beyond our means, and the root cause is an inability to delay our gratification. It's the "I want it now and I want it right now" attitude. We tend to spend money on unnecessary things on a whim. We put things that we want on credit when we probably don't need to be buying those items in the first place.

It's clear how this kind of a relationship with money can set us up for marital strife. The best remedy is to observe how your partner spends his or her money on little things. Do they wait for a good deal, or do they make spontaneous decisions? Do they have the mentality of "I deserve this," or are they more in the ballpark of "I've worked for this, and so therefore I'm going to treat myself this one time"?

I make these comments because making an occasional splurge isn't bad. But if you view money and possessions as a means to happiness, then you're in for a rough future! So, pay attention to your potential life mate. Does she have an expensive purse, but no money in it? Is he driving a flashy car, but borrows from you to pay for gas? Is he or she saving for retirement? Does he or she have a plan for emergency situations? Watch out for the little things, because they can point to much bigger problems under the surface.

You Are Not Your Net Worth

As you go through this exercise, however, you may realize that *you* are the one with the financial issues—not your partner! You may experience shame when you can't afford the things that others can afford. You may feel pressure to achieve a certain lifestyle, thinking that this will bring friends, happiness, and status. Or you may view every pay raise as an excuse to up your level of living. You may feel as though you deserve to have bigger and bigger homes and more and more flashier vehicles to drive. You may not realize the root problem of that kind of a mindset.

If this is you, take heart. You can begin to implement change today. In order to free your mind, you need to change the way you think about money. You need to realize that it's what you keep that counts. The Bible says that those who gather little by little shall increase what they have (Proverbs 13:11).

Below are four family finance principles to help change your mindset about money:

1. Financial prosperity is a process, not an event.
The hardest part of achieving a state of financial health is that you have to recognize that it is a journey—it takes time. You also have to recognize that your attitude about money is much more important than how much you earn.

Successful people don't just happen overnight. The people around you who seem to always have enough probably weren't handed that kind of a life situation. They very likely put in the hard work and made sacrifices to get there.

Once you realize that financial success and stability is a journey, then you will start to see that there is no shame in having less than other people have. Everyone starts somewhere, so don't be embarrassed to start slow. As long as you have a plan and you implement it, the rest will work itself out.

2. We are God's stewards. Being responsible enough to leave an inheritance for the next generation just so happens to be part of God's plan. The book of Proverbs says, "A good man leaveth an inheritance to his children; and the wealth of the sinner is laid up for the righteous" (13:22).

God expects us to leave enough, not only for our children, but also for our grandchildren. He expects this because He expects us to be smart with that which He gives us. He expects us to invest wisely and make sound business decisions. He also expects us to understand that wealth and material possessions are not truly ours anyway. All good things come from Him (James 1:17).

This is important, not only because it puts things in perspective, but also because it protects the people we love. Being a good steward means having enough to cover the expenses of our funerals. It means not leaving the people we love with no means of supporting themselves. It means looking out for our spouses and children if we die.

You can't take your possessions to the grave, and they certainly will not buy you a ticket into heaven. Instead, leave your wealth behind for your offspring and be open about discussing with them what they should do should anything happen to you.

3. How you handle your money reflects how you handle your life. Your finances can be spent, saved, squandered, or invested. Though we all engage in each of these strategies, we usually gravitate heavily toward one or two of them. So, which ones most define you?

I have found that the way a person handles his or her money is often the way they handle their life. Some people constantly spend their resources and energy on temporary things; others save up their resources and energy and never truly engage with the world; others squander their lives and use it on things that don't matter, or they don't contribute to the greater good; and still others invest their lives in achieving the maximum amount of impact that they can while they are here.

As you dig into your relationship with money, think about how it reflects the way you live your own life. And then consider any changes you need to make to alter that course.

4. Money is a tool, a test, and a testimony. A financial increase is always a wonderful blessing from God, but it also comes with huge responsibility. Every "payday" is an opportunity for God to see where your priorities lie. He is looking to see whether you tithe, save, spend, or give. I always recommend that 10 percent of your income go toward tithing, 10 percent go into your savings, and 80 percent cover your costs of living. For me, that has proven to be a simple baseline for how I handle financial blessings that I receive.

Manage It Right

After you change your mindset using the above principles, you can change your actions and the way you manage your money. Here are a few tips on how to decrease your spending so that you can increase your investing and saving, and begin to live within your means.

Spot areas of instant gratification. It's the curse of modern times—that feeling that you need it *now*. But no, you don't. Children of God live with a different mentality. They know that everything God has promised them is going to happen at the right time, and they realize that having something does not make or break their calling, their future, or their happiness. Patience is part of the process of learning how to manage your finances the right way.

Learn how to be content. An important aspect of managing your need for instant gratification is to learn how to be happy with the things you already have. God has already blessed you in many ways, and learning to be content with that blessing will take you far toward being less antsy, less focused on status, and more grateful and positive in life.

Perform plastic surgery. No, not on your face. On your credit cards. Credit cards can be very costly, so it's important not to use them unless you can afford to pay the debt off in full without any added interest or fees.

If you're struggling with limiting your credit card purchases, consider cutting up your plastic credit cards so that the temptation isn't there at all. This will prevent you from spending money you don't have and keep you from wasting your hard-earned cash on interest and banking fees.

My wife and I have taken an approach to credit cards that has served us well over the years. A while ago, we agreed to use our credit card only for little things here and there, and only when we knew that we could pay it off right away. Most of the time, we have paid for purchases with cash or with debit cards. But we didn't implement this strategy until we found ourselves in debt and with no money on hand! We knew we needed to change our approach to our money, so credit cards became almost nonexistent to us. Consequently, we don't waste money on interest and fees, and we're now a lot happier with our financial position.

Pay it off. When we first married, there was a period of time when we only had one car. It was hard, but we managed. We managed because we wanted to go about getting a second car the right way. Instead of taking out an expensive loan, we set aside money month after month. Eventually, we were able to buy that second car, and we paid cash for it!

Another tip to avoid loans like this is to think about long-term maintenance. Sure, you might be able to afford that car payment, but can you also afford the monthly maintenance and insurance for the new vehicle? If it breaks down, will you be able to handle the bills? This applies to everything that we buy. From our homes to our wardrobes, we must be able to pay off any loans quickly and handle any financial repercussions that those items may bring. If we can't do those two things, then we need to consider either saving up more money before making the purchase or opting for a less expensive item.

Have an emergency fund. Almost half of Americans don't have more than $100 set aside in case of an emergency.[5] But think about it…what kind of an emergency only costs $100?! Though $100 is a good place to start, an emergency savings account should be a part of your budget that you really want to get under control sooner rather than later, because you don't want an emergency requiring you to dig out those credit cards that you have worked so hard to set aside.

Place your emergency funds in a safe place or in a savings account. Ideally, you should have three to six months' costs of living saved up. That may sound like a lot, but it's so important! Don't leave yourself and your family vulnerable to the next economic depression or a job loss. Start saving now. Show that you can be wise in the little things.

Don't fall for scams. Prosperity is a process, and patience is part of it. It's tempting to sign up for a pyramid scheme or a too-good-to-be-true investment opportunity, but that just isn't how building wealth works. Get a decent job, work hard, and build your finances from there.

Learn how to be cute on your level. You can be beautiful and happy with yourself however little you have. God made you beautiful, with beautiful skin that protects you from the environment, eyes that can see His world, and ears that can hear His Word. Recognizing your natural beauty is the first step toward realizing that you don't need the most expensive perfume or a membership at the country club to be worth it.

So, stop pretending to be someone you're not, living on a level that isn't conducive to your actual earnings. Scale it back. Live on your level, and enjoy your life by simply being you.

Pay your dues. Whether it's taxes, bills, or tithes, make it a point to pay your dues first. By setting aside that money and planning around it, you can create a realistic game plan of how to best use any other leftover funds.

The Importance of Planning

Jesus said, "For which of you, desiring to build a tower, doth not first sit down and count the cost, whether he have wherewith to complete it?" (Luke 14:28).

In order to follow a life of financial stewardship and achieve financial happiness, you need to plan for it. You need to work for it. You need a strategy in place. But sometimes marriage messes that up. When two people with differing financial goals come together, it can prove to be problematic.

It's important to come to an agreement on finances and how to handle them. Only then can you both move forward into a life of sound financial decisions and good stewardship of what God has blessed you with.

Chapter Seven Questions

Question: Why is it particularly important for a couple to be agreed about finances prior to marriage? If there are areas of disagreement, how should they be handled?

_____

_____

_____

_____

_____

_____

_____

_____

_____

_____

Question: What are the heart attitudes necessary to avoid debt, live within limited means, give when you don't have what you want, and save for needed purchases?

_____

_____

_____

_____

_____

_____

_____

_____

_____

_____

_____

Question: "Financial prosperity is a process, not an event." If you are dating or engaged, do you see your significant other as helping or hindering that process? What practical choices does each of you need to make to move toward ultimately leaving an inheritance to your children and grandchildren?

_____

_____

_____

_____

_____

_____

_____

_____

_____

_____

_____

_____

Action: Talk to your pastor about financial stewardship courses that you can take through the church or the community. This is a wonderful activity for any seriously dating or engaged couple to do together.

Chapter Seven Notes

CHAPTER EIGHT

Work Together

Every man setteth on first the good wine; and when men
have drunk freely, then that which is worse: thou hast kept
the good wine until now.

—John 2:10

Have you ever met one of those couples who are cele-
brating their fortieth, fiftieth, or even sixtieth wedding
anniversary?

Amazing, isn't it?! What I love most about these special couples is the fact that when you ask them what the
key to a happy, long-lasting marriage is, they all give you
the same advice, no matter what country they came from,
what their skin color is, what their income level is, or how
many kids they've had.

What is their advice? How did they keep things going
for such a long time? I'm glad you asked!

It Takes Two

Do you remember the Bible story of the wedding in Cana, where the host ran out of wine (John 2:1-11.)? When Jesus heard what had happened, He asked that jars be filled with water. Once that was done, He blessed the water and turned it into the best wine the guests had ever tasted (John 2:7-10).

Jesus didn't perform this miracle all on His own. He utilized others to achieve His goal. He directed the servants to fill waterpots with water and to draw it out of the pots. As they obediently responded to His direction, the water was turned to wine. The bottom line here is that no one can make a relationship successful by themselves. It takes two to tango, two to tie a knot, and two to make it work.

Anything worth having requires some effort, and a successful marriage is no exception. It takes work on both of your parts to keep things together. Once you say the words "I do" in God's presence, you are committed to doing whatever it takes to make the relationship work. You're agreeing to be bound by the covenant of marriage, and it's up to you to make it a positive blessing in your life.

Five Components of a Strong Marriage

Once you accept that you have your own role to play in the success of your relationship, then it's time to take a look at the factors that determine a happy marriage.

The secret ingredients that will keep a marriage good

for years are not so secret! In fact, we have already covered some of these to an extent already, but repetition is always good for our memory, so let's go over them again.

Adaptability

A marriage does not run on a German train timetable. A lot of things can happen unexpectedly and usually at the worst possible time. You have to be able to go with the flow and adapt to a changing environment. Yes, you should plan, but you also need to recognize that your plans will likely have to be tossed aside every now and then.

I learned the importance of adaptability early on in my marriage. My wife and I have two children. We were very well prepared for the first one to come along, but, of course, there were things we had to learn (as is usually is the case with your first child). When the second baby came along, though, we thought it'd be so much easier. We figured that we had done it all before, and that we were prepared and experienced. We thought wrong. Nothing can prepare you for a child with special needs.

This was definitely an unplanned part of life. We had to adjust quickly, and there were some tough times. After all, 80 percent of marriages end in divorce when a child with special needs is born. We had to learn to adapt, or we would become another statistic.

You will also face many challenges throughout your marriage. Be flexible. Understand that it's good to plan, but that the plan sometimes doesn't pan out. Learn how to adapt in the face of adversity and band together rather than fight with each other.

Empathy

I've talked about the importance of getting to know to each other during the dating phase, but what really helps speed this process up is when you learn to feel for the other person—when you learn empathy.

Empathy is the ability to put yourself in the other person's shoes and walk with him or her patiently through whatever difficulty might arise. It's seeing things from their perspective instead of remaining an outsider looking in. Empathy is crucial to becoming a unified team.

Problem-Solving Skills

Marriage is full of unexpected issues popping up here and there, and the faster you learn how to problem-solve *together*, the sooner you'll learn how to pull out of those hard times.

Talk through your problems. Support one another. Arrive at a solution together. Do these things, and you'll make it through whatever roadblock comes your way. And while you're out looking for a potential spouse, consider finding someone with great critical thinking skills. That will come in handy a whole lot more than, say, good looks will in the years to come.

Emotional Stability

This is a serious one, I know, but it's also crucial. Without emotional stability, it's hard to come to agreements, to problem-solve, to understand and empathize, and to adapt. Emotional stability is the cornerstone of a healthy marriage, and it's a necessity for personal growth.

An excellent sign of emotional maturity is the ability to handle difficult and emotional situations—particularly situations that could bring about anger with each other. Life is hard and unfair, and we all get angry from time to time. But it's one thing to get frustrated and to feel that anger coming over you. It's another to keep it under control and manage it in a calm, respectful way.

Anger can manifest itself in verbal or physical ways. So think about the words you say. And watch your actions. The way you handle anger is a reflection of your morals, just as much as it's a reflection of your inner stability. As the Bible says: "Make no friendship with a man that is given to anger" (Proverbs 22:24).

Effective Communication Skills

I'm convinced there should be compulsory training in this skill—it's that important to a marriage and to every other human relationship on the planet.

Ask any happily married person their key for success, or ask any divorcée what ultimately led to the end of their relationship, and they will both answer the same: good communication (or in the divorcée's case, likely the lack thereof).

It's not rocket science. It simply boils down to being able to listen to the other person, to truly understand what they mean, before you insert your opinion or your thoughts into the discussion. It's about listening before you speak. And it's about choosing careful words that are clear and honest.

Communication is important in your relationship with God, too. We need to be able to talk with Him and listen for His voice. We need that open dialogue rather than just a flood of our own thoughts and feelings.

The Great News

Here's the tough news: Even if the two of you come together, willing and ready to work on your relationship, that alone is not going to be enough.

Marriage is a collision of two separate histories. Every person comes to the table with their own talents, strengths, and weaknesses, but they also bring their own baggage. A few vows at the altar don't change who you are and the complexity of your upbringing. The simple act of getting married isn't enough to make a marriage work. And you can put to work all of the five good ingredients listed above and still face extreme hardships that will threaten to pull you apart.

The good news? There is one certain magical ingredient that can make the impossible possible—and that is God.

I have seen it firsthand as a pastor and a marriage counselor. Anything is possible with the help of the Holy Spirit. A relationship that is dead can be revived. And a relationship that has two people who very desperately want to keep it together can be strengthened.

Your marriage will need supernatural help. You'll need God's blessing and His Spirit to guide you each and every day—when things are easy and when they're tough. And every difficulty you encounter needs to be resolved God's way.

Tough Decisions

We've talked a lot about how to tackle the most difficult aspects of marriage, but what if, in reading this book, you've started to wonder if maybe you've made a bad choice? What if you're starting to think that you might already be in a bad relationship?

If you're at this kind of a crossroads in your marriage or another relationship, you have to ask yourself the following questions:

1. Has my love for God changed because of this relationship? Has this man/woman brought me closer or led me further away from God?

2. Do I still obey God's voice? Am I still following His principles and living a life that He wants me to live?

In short, has your commitment to the Lord and His Word increased or decreased as a result of being in this relationship?

The right person will always make you want to love God and serve Him more. And if you and the person with whom you are in a relationship are "unequally yoked," if you differ too much when it comes to your beliefs and your moral standards, then you will face extreme hardship, because you will have two different perspectives holding on to the same rope and pulling it in different directions.

I am praying for you if this is where you are right now. There are no easy answers if you have already taken marriage vows. But if you are still in the dating phase, and if the questions above challenged you at all, I urge you to reconsider marriage to that person.

Commit to One Another Today

Just like Jesus produced the best wine ever at the wedding in Cana of Galilee, with His help, you can have the best marriage ever. Follow God's Word. Be prepared. Remember that it takes two people walking in agreement to succeed. And know that if you strive to love Him and follow Him and love one another, He will come through for you. He will see to it that the best is yet to come.

WORKBOOK

Chapter Eight Questions

Question: Are you an adaptable person? Think back to the last time that life didn't go the way you planned or expected. How did you handle it? How can you grow in your ability to adapt to interruptions, delays, and difficulties?

_____

_____

_____

_____

_____

_____

_____

_____

_____

_____

_____

Question: How do you and your partner solve problems? Do you work together or pull apart? What are steps you can take to be a united team next time you face a problem?

_____

_____

_____

_____

_____

_____

_____

_____

_____

_____

_____

Question: Why does every marriage need supernatural help? What are some ways in which couples can keep a spiritual dimension to their relationship?

_____

_____

_____

_____

_____

_____

_____

_____

_____

_____

_____

_____

_____

Action: Take a personality type assessment (if you are dating or married, do this as a couple). What are the communication strengths and weaknesses inherent with your personality type and that of your significant other? How do your personality types typically interact? Use what you have learned to help build stronger communication skills.

Chapter Eight Notes

_____

_____

_____

_____

_____

_____

_____

_____

_____

_____

_____

_____

_____

_____

_____

_____

_____

_____

_____

_____

_____

_____

CHAPTER NINE

Raise Them Right

Tend the flock of God which is among you, exercising the oversight, but willingly, according to the will of God; nor yet for filthy lucre, but of a ready mind: neither as lording it over the charge allotted to you, but making yourselves ensamples to the flock.

—1 Peter 5:2-3

The Bible says that it is God's will for us to "be fruitful, and multiply, and replenish the earth" (Genesis 1:28). *Sounds good to me!* You might be thinking, *I can't wait to have kids!*

While the thought of having mini-versions of yourself and your spouse can be thrilling and fun, I want you to think more long term. How will you ensure that you raise your children in a godly way? How will you tend to your own flock?

There is a saying that "it takes a village to raise a child," but I believe that our communities are only as strong as the families we are building. Having God in your family makes it stronger. Following His ways makes it stronger. Practicing His love makes it stronger. And what's even more crucial to note is that His principles can apply to all families: atheist, agnostic, and more. So even if you're on the fence with the whole God thing, you can still apply His parenting tips to your personal approach.

Agreement Is Power

Before we proceed, I again must stress the importance of being in agreement with your spouse in this area. As with many other things I've covered in this book, agreement is a position of power. Arriving at a consensus and deciding together that you are going to follow X kind of rules or handle a situation in a Z kind of way is so imperative. You need to get to a point where you both are reasonably happy with your strategies and your solutions.

I have met many young couples who were doing really well together, until they had their first child. Then, coupled with the stress and joy of being a parent, came a wave of arguments over what should be done and how with little Johnny.

This stress many times can be avoided if you simply talk about your parenting styles before you have children or before you get married. Share your experience of childhood and how your parents' parenting style worked or didn't work for you. Spend some time together with your little nephews and nieces to see how your ideas and strategies work in practice.

While there is no way to know exactly how you are

going to be as a parent before you actually become a parent, it's worthwhile to discuss your beliefs, your attitudes, and your prior experience with child care with your other half.

This is particularly important if you are bringing any children from a previous relationship into a new marriage.

In the modern world, blended families are becoming more and more common, but they still bring a host of new and different challenges that didn't come up in the previous relationship.

Your kid misbehaves, and you never correct him.
You only look out for your kids and not mine.
You are too hard on my child.

These are some of the issues that I see blended families facing today. It's hard to parent your own children; it's even harder to share parenting responsibilities in a blended family.

So, make it a point to discuss any parenting issues or questions. Come to an agreement on strategies. Understand that you need to create a new family in which everyone is loved and treated equally by everyone else.

Principles for Raising Godly Children

Now that I've laid the groundwork, I want to launch into what I believe are the most crucial components of raising children up to love and follow God, and to treat others with love and respect—and many of these principles start with you setting the example.

1. Teach your children how to speak respectfully.
It's so hard to deal with a child who talks back and has no respect for his or her elders. But here's a truth: He or she didn't get that way on their own. To raise a child who is respectful, then you must model respectful behavior to others in front of them.

Your words are a reflection of your morals, and your mouth tells on your character (Matthew 12:34). Kids pick up on this stuff quickly. They can spot a "do what I say, not what I do" situation a mile away. Rather, it should always be "do as I do." When we lead by example, kids fall in line.

Be a role model for your child by not swearing and by being respectful toward other people (including your children!). Learn how to manage your emotions and your frustrations in particular. If you can do it in a mature way, your children—who are always watching you—will learn it from you.

2. Teach them self-control. As you have probably understood so far, the key to successfully managing mature relationships in a godly way is the ability to control your impulses. Self-control is an awesome tool, and it is also a very important factor in achieving whatever goals in life we have. Studies have shown that the ability to delay gratification and keep yourself in check is more likely to lead to success than a college degree will (and it's way cheaper!).[6]

If you want your children to be happy and achieve their goals in life, if you want them to have good lives and blessed relationships, then teach them self-control. Do not give them what they want whenever they want it. Rather, teach them that there are times in life when we just can't have the things we want. And there are other times when, if we wait long enough, we eventually see that blessing come through.

3. Don't raise lazy people. I hear many parents say "I would do anything for my children." This desire to make sacrifices for your kids is a good thing, but be careful with it becoming corrupted. "I would do anything for my children" should never become "I do everything for my children."

There is a trap in the "do everything for your children" mentality, and that is the risk of raising lazy people. There is nothing worse than a cute, lazy teenager. They have no standards, and they are likely to end up being dumped, jobless, or doing dodgy stuff, living ungodly lives. They have no drive, no ambition, and their only goal in life is to hit the movies on the weekends or see how much spending money they can get from their mom or dad.

If you're a single mother working two jobs to put your son through college and you come home to find your fifteen-year-old "baby" sitting on the couch playing video games while the garbage is stinking to seventh heaven, then you, my friend, have a lazy teenager. And a big problem!

We need to teach our kids how to chip in, how to do their part, and how to appreciate what they've been given. This needs to be taught to kids who come from a lot and to kids who come from nothing. Teach them by example how to have motivation for life, how to problem-solve, how to plan their next steps with God's guidance, how to respect hard work and find value in it beyond a paycheck. Do this and you will raise awesome contributors to society.

4. Don't expect other people to do your parenting job for you. Badly behaved kids? Lazy ones? Good-for-nothing? And whose fault is this? The school's? The teachers'? The church's? No. Your responsibility as a parent is to raise your children in a godly way, no matter how many bad examples they run into while out in the world.

It's up to you to teach them proper behavior and control. It's up to you to instill morals and ethics in them. It's up to you to show them the rules for living a God-blessed life. It's on you, Mom or Dad.

5. Give your children the right environment in which to grow. Because outside influences are so powerful, it's important to make sure that you create a safe and constructive environment or home in which your kids can grow up.

If you're unhappy in your marriage, if you're a victim of domestic violence, abuse, or substance use, think about your children as well as your own happiness and well-being. Yes, you are bound by the covenant of marriage, but you are also responsible for your kids. Don't allow your children to be damaged by an incredibly sinful environment. If you're with a man or a woman whose ungodly behavior and actions threaten you and the kids, take appropriate action.

It's your role to seek a safe space for your family—

even if that means stepping away from your spouse for a while.

It's on You

Parenting is one of the hardest jobs in the world: It makes you lose your sleep, question your sanity, and do all sorts of weird things you'd never thought you'd do. And you do all of it to help your kids become happy, healthy, good people.

Seeing your children grow up to become responsible, mature, and positive adults who follow God's Word is the biggest reward. This is the job given to you by God, so you'd better do your best to prepare for it! Sure, there will be surprises along the way. But if you can get your foundation down and come to an agreement on the basics, then most of the battle is already won.

WORKBOOK

Chapter Nine Questions

Question: What are some things that couples can do prior to having children to help them prepare to be on the same page about parenting?

_____

_____

_____

_____

_____

_____

_____

_____

_____

_____

_____

Question: What qualities do parents need to build into their children to help them succeed and be a blessing to others? What are specific, practical ways to instill these qualities?

_____

_____

_____

_____

_____

_____

_____

_____

_____

_____

_____

Question: How would you describe the "right environment" for raising children? Is your vision similar to your partner's vision?

_____

_____

_____

_____

_____

_____

_____

_____

_____

_____

_____

_____

Action: Interview parents of young children, elementary-aged children, and teenagers. (You might also talk to parents in a blended family if this is or will be your situation.) Ask each couple about how this stage of parenting impacts their marriage and how they work together as a team to parent their kids.

Chapter Nine Notes

CONCLUSION

God Is the Glue

And above all these things put on love, which is the bond of perfectness.
—*Colossians 3:14*

No other dimension of the human experience has been pondered, discussed, debated, analyzed, and dreamed about more than the subject of love.

But our Western culture got it wrong: love is not a feeling. Feelings come and go. They change and are subject to health, finances, life events, and so much more. Anything based on a feeling is going to be unstable. That's why if you want to find true, lasting love, look beyond the emotion of the moment. Go deeper and look for commitment.

Remember what I said in the beginning of the book? There are four types of love, and the English language puts them all in the same basket, labeling them with the same word. But other languages have many different words for the different types of love we experience. The

Bible has *eros*, or a sexual desire; *filia*, or brotherly love; *storge*, or parental affection; and *agape*, the highest level of love—the love of God for man and of man for God.

Agape means being one with God. When you love someone with *agape* love, you look for unity with them, and you consider them and do things for their benefit and not yours. *Agape* love never changes. It's self-initiating, it's consistent, it's proactive, and it's adaptable. It's *agape* love that you should dedicate your time and energy toward seeking and developing.

Love Is Not Enough

But your work doesn't stop once you find that true love. It doesn't stop with the wedding or the marriage license. All of that is actually the easiest part! Once you are married, then the true hard work really sets in. This is when you need to come together more than ever and put into play all of the things that you discussed during the dating phase—all of those points of agreement. This is where the rubber meets the road.

And then, day after day, it's about holding fast to those points of agreement. It's about continuing to work through the bad times and thank God for the good times. It's about recognizing that marriage is a work in progress.

If you hold fast to the truth of God's Word, then there is good news for you. You have a secret weapon. God is the glue that will hold a relationship together. He is the anchor for your marriage. As long as you both are leaning on Him and seeking Him in your relationship, those trials don't stand a chance.

In times of struggle, you know where to seek guidance and consolation. And in times of disagreement, you know where to go to get God's opinion on the matter.

Yes, marriage is hard, but God will help you navigate this most amazing and powerful relationship—and do it in agreement.

This Is Just the Beginning

After reading this book, I hope you feel better equipped to date, marry, and raise children. I hope you have a clearer understanding of what it takes to find a love that lasts, a love that embraces you the way you are and helps you become a better person in God's eyes.

I hope you now have a handle on what to avoid, *whom* to avoid, and for what you should be looking. I hope you understand the seriousness of these life choices, and I hope you understand that even a bad decision can be turned around for God's glory.

If God calls you to be married, the only way to make it work is to build that commitment with God as your Guide. He loves you so much. He gave you His Son, who died for your sins and for your shame. God showed you and He continues to show you the love that never changes, that keeps loving you even when you fail, the love that leads to eternal happiness.

God is love. And He wants you to experience His love in marriage, His love as a parent, and His love for your brothers and sisters. It is our duty to strive to get it right, to do our part on this journey and aim high.

Keep your standards. Seek *agape* love. Come to an

agreement on important issues. And lean on Him for the rest.

REFERENCES

Notes

1. Maner, Gary. *Aistheterion*. Xulon Press, 2008.

2. Saxon, Joshua. "Why Your Customers' Attention is the Scarcest Resource in 2017." *American Marketing Association*. https://www.ama.org/partners/content/Pages/why-customers-attention-scarcest-resources-2017.aspx.

3. "Internet Pornography by the Numbers; a Significant Threat to Society." *Webroot*. https://www.webroot.com/us/en/resources/tips-articles/internet-pornography-by-the-numbers.

4. El Issa, Erin. "2017 American Household Credit Card Debt Study." *Nerd Wallet*. https://www.nerdwallet.com/blog/average-credit-card-debt-household.

5. Huddleston, Cameron. "Most Americans Lack Savings to Pay for These Huge Emergencies." *Chicago Tribune*. February 8, 2018. http://www.chicagotribune.com/business/ct-biz-emergency-savings-

personal-finance-20180208-story.html.

6. Lickerman, Alex. "The Power of Delaying Gratification." *Psychology Today.* July 29, 2012. https://www.psychologytoday.com/us/blog/happiness-in-world/201207/the-power-delaying-gratification.

About the Author

Pastor John F. Ramsey Sr. is the gifted and anointed founder and senior pastor of New Life Worship Center, an exciting and rapidly growing church located in Indianapolis, Indiana. He ministers with power while using humor to make often complex biblical concepts enjoyable, simple, relevant, and practical.

Ramsey attended Fort Wayne Public Schools and graduated from Snider High School. Following graduation, inspired by his love of athletics, he accepted a football scholarship at Miami University of Ohio and began pursuing a major in education. During his junior year, at the age of 21, he accepted

God's call to the ministry. It was during these college years that he began readying himself to do the will of God on a full-time basis.

In 2001 God called Pastor Ramsey and his wife, Alicia, to open New Life Worship Center with the help of Eastern Star Church. Pastor Ramsey developed a central theme for New Life Worship Center: *"A Local Church with a Global Vision."* Pastor Ramsey and the New Life Worship Center family are fully positioned to reach God's people on a local, regional, national, and international basis.

As it grew, New Life Worship Center moved from its initial, 350-seat sanctuary (Kessler location) into a new main location—a 13-acre, 80,000-square-foot, 1,400-seat facility in the city's historic Traders Point neighborhood—in July 2005. Since its inception, the church has grown to over 5,000 members with 30 active ministries. To more effectively serve the Indianapolis community, in 2007 New Life Worship Center also completed the cash purchase of a central campus location at 3425 Boulevard Place in Center Township.

Pastor Ramsey serves as mentor and spiritual father to a number of local pastors. He is blessed to serve under Bishop I.V. Hilliard of New Light Christian Center in Houston, Texas, as his spiritual father. Pastor Ramsey is a much sought-after preacher and a featured national keynote speaker for various leadership and development programs. He is a member of the Association of Independent Ministries. God's anointing has enabled Pastor Ramsey to bring some of the nation's leading pastors, teachers, and recording artists to New Life Worship Center to bless the congregation and the Indianapolis community each year. He also consults at Taylor University regarding diversity and leadership and as a ministry mentor.

Pastor Ramsey is most passionate about helping families to become stronger. Known for his anointing in the areas of faith, relationships, and financial stewardship, he is the author of *Smart Money Management: A Biblical Approach to Financial Stability*, *Armed and Dangerous: Equipping Leaders for Effective Ministry*, and now *One Night Stand*. He is also the co-author of a highly regarded book entitled *About My Father's Business: Merging Industry and Ministry*.

Pastor Ramsey is married to his lovely wife, Alicia, and they are the proud parents of three wonderful children: a daughter, Judah Maree, and sons Jeremiah David and John Jr.

About Sermon To Book

SermonToBook.com began with a simple belief: that sermons should be touching lives, *not* collecting dust. That's why we turn sermons into high-quality books that are accessible to people all over the globe.

Turning your sermon series into a book exposes more people to God's Word, better equips you for counseling, accelerates future sermon prep, adds credibility to your ministry, and even helps make ends meet during tight times.

John 21:25 tells us that the world itself couldn't contain the books that would be written about the work of Jesus Christ. Our mission is to try anyway. Because in heaven, there will no longer be a need for sermons or books. Our time is now.

If God so leads you, we'd love to work with you on your sermon or sermon series.

Visit www.sermontobook.com to learn more.

91208322R00078

Made in the USA
San Bernardino, CA
25 October 2018